Contents

3A Assessment

Big Pants
page 2

3B Assessment

Freedom
page 14

3A written by
Dee Reid

3A illustrated by
Dylan Gibson

3B written by
Alison Hawes

3B illustrated by
Ollie Cuthbertson

Series editor **Dee Reid**

T0345369

Heinemann

Part of Pearson

Characters

Tariq

Tariq's mum

Imran

Tricky words

- launderette
- clothes
- machine
- someone
- everyone
- thought

Read these words to the student. Help them with these words when they appear in the text.

Introduction

Tariq is in the year above Imran at school. Sometimes they get on OK but sometimes Tariq likes to boss Imran around. One day Tariq had a cold and he didn't want to go to school. His mum made him go to the launderette instead.

BIG PANTS

Tariq had a cold.
He said to his mum, "I don't want to go to school, I have got a cold."

"If you don't go to school, you must go to the launderette," said his mum.

"Do I have to?" asked Tariq.
"School or launderette?" asked his mum.
"Launderette," said Tariq.

Tariq's mum put the clothes in a bag
and Tariq went to the launderette.

Tariq put the clothes in the machine.

"Nice pants!" said someone.
Tariq looked around.
Imran was laughing at Tariq's mum's pants.

"Are they your pants?" asked Imran.
"Get lost!" said Tariq. "They are not my pants."

"Why are you not at school?" asked Tariq.

"I have got a cold," said Imran.

"Me too!" said Tariq.

"Why are you at the launderette?" asked Imran.

"My mum said I had to go," said Tariq.

Imran said, "I think they are your pants.
I will tell everyone at school you have
big pink pants," and he laughed and laughed.

Tariq looked at Imran laughing.
I should have gone to school, Tariq thought.

Quiz ////////////////////////

Text comprehension

Literal comprehension
p3 Why did Tariq not want to go to school?
p4 What did Tariq's mum say he had to choose between?
p8 Why did Imran laugh at Tariq?
p10 Why was Imran at the launderette?
p11 What did Imran say he would do?

Inferential comprehension
p5 Why did Tariq's mum give him a choice between going to school and to the launderette?
p9 Do you think Imran really thinks the big pants belong to Tariq?
p12 Why did Tariq wish he had gone to school?

Personal response
- Would you have chosen to go to the launderette rather than school?
- Would you be embarrassed if something like this happened to you?

Spelling challenge

Study these words for one minute. Then write them from memory.

Phonically regular

them   this   will   then   help

Irregular

was   have   the   said   are

Ha! Ha! Ha!

What happened to the leopard that fell into the washing machine?

He came out spotless!

13

Characters

Salan

The King

Tricky words

- huge
- feathers
- basilisk

- afraid
- closer
- does

Read these words to the student. Help them with these words when they appear in the text.

Introduction

Salan is a slave. The evil King promised Salan his freedom if he did four difficult and dangerous tasks. Salan has done all the tasks. He has given the King all he wants so now Salan wants the King to set him free.

FREEDOM

Salan goes to see the King.
He wants the King to set him free.

"I have given you all you want," says Salan to the King. "Now you must set me free."

"No!" says the King. "I will not set you free."

"But I have given you the skin of the Lion of Jedda,"
says Salan.
"So you have," says the King.
"I have given you one of the Green Dragon's fangs,"
says Salan.
"So you have," says the King.

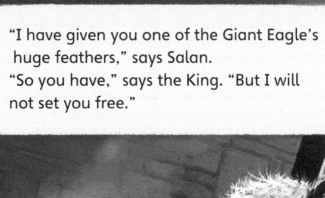

"I have given you one of the Giant Eagle's huge feathers," says Salan.
"So you have," says the King. "But I will not set you free."

"I am the King," says the King. "I can do as I like and I will not set you free."

But Salan is in luck!
He sees a bag. In the bag is the basilisk's head.
One look from a basilisk can turn you to stone.
Salan is not afraid. He has a plan to be free.
The King has not looked in the bag.
Now Salan will get the King to look at the basilisk's head.

"Come closer," says Salan to the King.

Salan takes the basilisk's head out of the bag.

Salan does not look at it but the King does!

The King turns to stone.
Now I am free, thinks Salan.

Quiz

Text comprehension

Literal comprehension
p16 What does Salan want from the King?
p19 Why does the King say he will not set Salan free?
p20 What is Salan's plan?
p20 What happens if you look at a basilisk?
p22 Why does Salan not turn to stone?

Inferential comprehension
p17 Why does Salan feel angry with the King?
p20 Is Salan brave?
p21 Why does Salan ask the King to come closer?

Personal response
• Do you think Salan is clever?
• Do you think the King deserves what happens to him?

Spelling challenge

Study these words for one minute. Then write them from memory.

Phonically regular

like   take   must   just   from

Irregular

want   look   they   give   come

Ha! Ha! Ha!

What happened when the lion ate the comedian?

He felt funny!